D1443288

What Makes Me A
CATHOLIC?

Adam Woog

**KIDHAVEN
PRESS**™

THOMSON

———✦———™

GALE

San Diego • Detroit • New York • San Francisco • Cleveland
New Haven, Conn. • Waterville, Maine • London • Munich

Special thanks to Mary Alice Tully and her loyal sidekicks Harold and Colin Elias—trusted friends and consultants in Catholicism and in many other areas of life as well.

© 2004 by KidHaven Press. KidHaven Press is an imprint of Thomson Gale, a part of the Thomson Corporation. Thomson is a trademark and Gale are registered trademarks used herein under license.

KidHaven™ and Thomson Learning™ are trademarks used herein under license.

For more information, contact
KidHaven Press
27500 Drake Rd.
Farmington Hills, MI 48331-3535
Or you can visit our Internet site at http://www.gale.com

LIBRARY OF CONGRESS CATALOGING-IN-PUBLICATION DATA

Woog, Adam, 1953–
   Catholic / by Adam Woog.
     v. cm. — (What makes me a?)
   Includes bibliographical references (p.   ).
   Summary: Discusses Catholicism, including how Catholicism began, what Catholics believe, how they practice their faith, and what holidays they celebrate.
   ISBN 0-7377-2268-1 (alk. paper)
   1. Catholic Church—Juvenile literature. [1. Catholic Church.] I. Title. II. Series.
   BX948.W66 2004
   282—dc22
                                              2003024345

Printed in the United States of America

CONTENTS

CHAPTER ONE

How Did My Religion Begin?

The Catholic Church is the first and oldest Christian religion. It started about two thousand years ago. It is also the largest of the Christian religions. It has about 1 billion members.

Like all Christians, Catholics base their religion on the life and teachings of Jesus Christ. Jesus' life and teachings are recorded in the first four books of the New Testament of the Bible. These books are called the Gospels. The Gospels are named for the men who wrote them. They are called Matthew, Mark, Luke, and John. All of them were followers of Jesus. They wrote these books years after he died.

For this reason, some scholars argue that the Gospels should not be taken literally. They wonder if the stories changed when they were written down. However, Catholics believe the Gospels were inspired by God and so are literal and true.

Jesus' Early Life

The writers of the Gospels recorded that Jesus was born to Mary, the wife of a carpenter named Joseph. Joseph and Mary were Jews who lived in Judea, roughly where Israel is today.

An angel told Mary that her child would be the Son of God. The Old Testament of the Bible, the ancient sacred text of the Jews, had long predicted the coming of this holy man. He was also called the Messiah. According to the Old Testament, the Messiah would lead the world to eternal peace.

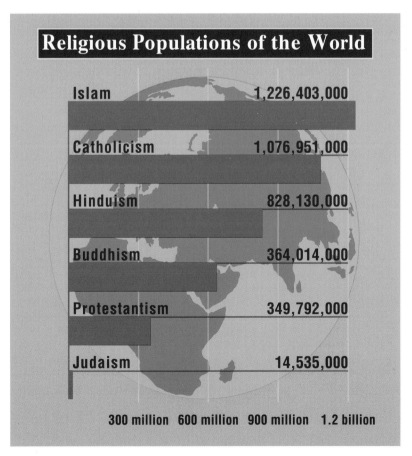

Religious Populations of the World

Islam	1,226,403,000
Catholicism	1,076,951,000
Hinduism	828,130,000
Buddhism	364,014,000
Protestantism	349,792,000
Judaism	14,535,000

300 million   600 million   900 million   1.2 billion

An angel tells Mary that her child will be the Son of God. The Old Testament predicted that Jesus would lead the world to eternal peace.

The writers of the Gospels record that one of Jesus' cousins, John the Baptist, recognized Jesus as the Messiah. John was a deeply religious man. He was also a prophet, someone who sees the future.

John got his name because he baptized people. That is, he used river water to ritually cleanse them of bad deeds, or sins. According to the Gospels, Jesus began preaching soon after John baptized him.

Spreading the Word

The Gospels note that Jesus' sermons attracted many followers, or disciples. Twelve men were especially close to Jesus. They were called apostles. All of Jesus' followers believed that he truly was the Son of God.

The writers of the Gospels summarize Jesus' message as, "You shall love your God above all things and your neighbor as yourself." They write that Jesus called himself a servant of God and that he said other people should be God's servants too. He said that if they

Jesus gives sight to a blind man. Jesus performed many miracles helping the sick and the disabled.

believed in God and lived good lives, their souls would have eternal peace in Heaven.

The Gospels record many of the parables Jesus told. These were simple stories that contained deep truths. The Gospels also say that Jesus performed miracles. He healed the sick and disabled. He fed thousands with just five loaves of bread and two fishes. He even brought a man back from the dead.

Killed and Resurrected

Jesus attracted many followers, but he also made enemies. The Gospels record these troubles. The Jewish religious leaders in Judea were angered by Jesus' claim to be the Messiah. Many people had made this claim, and the religious leaders saw no reason to believe him.

Meanwhile, the Roman political authorities in control of the region distrusted Jesus. He attracted many followers. The Roman authorities saw this as a threat to their own power. The Gospels say that Roman soldiers arrested Jesus. He was then sentenced to die. He was hung on a cross, or crucified. His body was then placed in a tomb. However, according to the Gospels, three days later the tomb was empty. Jesus had risen from the dead.

The Gospels say that Jesus spent another forty days on Earth. During this time, his disciples saw and spoke with him. Then he rose to Heaven to rejoin God.

The Church Forms

In the months and years after Jesus' death, his close followers began to spread the word that Jesus was the

Jesus made enemies among the people. Because he was a threat to their power, they executed him by hanging him on a cross.

Messiah. They also spoke of his teachings to all who would listen.

Little by little, a new religion began to grow. The growth and spread of this religion came about largely because of Saul (later called Paul) of Tarsus. Paul lived in the first century. At first he had opposed the early

The Cradle of Christianity

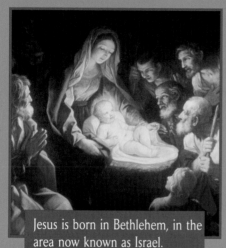

Jesus is born in Bethlehem, in the area now known as Israel.

Lake Huleh

Capernaum

Sea of Galilee

• Nazareth

• Caesarea

Mediterranean Sea

• Samaria

Jordan River

• Jaffa

• Lydda

Jericho •

Jerusalem •

Bethlehem •

Gaza •

JUDEA   • Hebron   *Dead Sea*

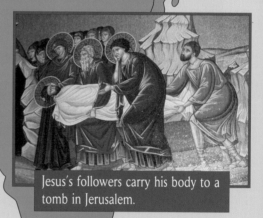

Jesus's followers carry his body to a tomb in Jerusalem.

Jesus rides into Jerusalem on a donkey, surrounded by his followers.

Present-day Israel

Christians. However, Jesus appeared to him in a powerful vision. After that, Paul proclaimed his devotion to Jesus. He and others like him brought Jesus' message to people around the world.

Spreading Around the World

Over the next centuries, Christianity spread very far. Many people were hunted down and punished, or persecuted, because of their beliefs. Within a few hundred years, however, Catholicism had grown to be one of the world's major religions. The church, headquartered in Rome, Italy, dominated religious life across Europe and in large sections of Asia and North Africa.

During the Middle Ages, roughly from the sixth to the fifteenth centuries, the church was one of the most powerful forces in Europe. In addition to spiritual guidance for its millions of followers, the church played a major role in keeping writing and other aspects of culture alive. Also, the church sent missionaries with the explorers of the fifteenth and sixteenth centuries, such as those who traveled to Africa and the Americas. These missionaries began churches in newly discovered lands. Millions more accepted the Catholic religion.

In these earliest years of the church, its leaders had developed a complex and carefully defined structure to pass on religious instruction and authority. Much of this time-honored structure remains today, almost completely unchanged.

CHAPTER TWO

How Is My Religion Organized?

O ne of the biggest differences between the Catholic Church and other Christian religions is the church's structure. This structure is very old. Much of it remains almost unchanged after two thousand years.

In Catholicism, all religious knowledge and inspiration is passed from a central point outward into a well-established organization. The center of the church thus directly connects to all of the Catholics around the world.

The Pope

The central figure is a religious leader called the pope. To Catholics, the pope is more than a leader. He is believed to be divinely inspired when speaking on matters of faith or morals. That means his influence comes directly from God. No other Christian religion has someone in as high and authoritative a position as the pope. He is unique.

The pope is the main source of spiritual knowledge, inspiration, and guidance for Catholics. He maintains the laws of the church, and he regularly issues new statements about religious matters. Everything he says about religious matters is considered infallible, meaning it cannot be wrong.

Popes are elected for life. When a pope dies, a new one is appointed by a special group of church leaders

Popes, like John Paul II, are elected for life.

called cardinals. Traditionally, this group chooses the new pope from among its own members.

The pope lives in the Vatican. This is a small country within Rome, Italy. Although the Vatican's main purpose is to be the center of the Catholic Church, it has a separate government like a country. In fact, it is the world's smallest country. It is only about 0.2 square miles in size and has fewer than one thousand residents. (Several thousand more people work there but live in Rome.)

The Vatican, located within Rome, Italy, is the world's smallest country.

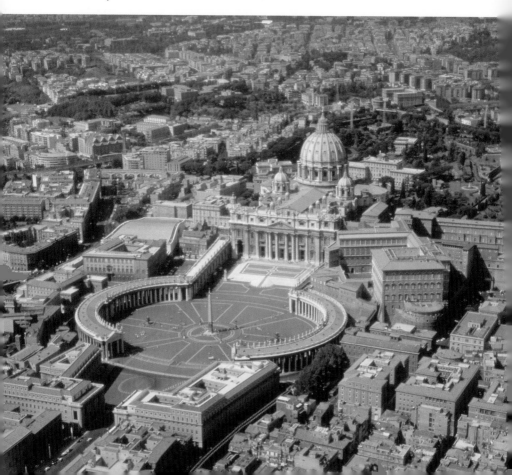

Below the pope in the church structure are archbishops and bishops. According to Catholic tradition, the pope and these bishops are in a direct line of authority that began with the apostles. This unbroken line of authority is called the Apostolic Succession.

It gives the pope and his bishops the authority to be the church's main leaders. The links in a direct spiritual chain continue even further. They form a connection between the pope and the rest of the Catholic Church.

Priests

Archbishops and bishops are in charge of archdioceses and dioceses. These are large geographical sections of the church's authority. Each diocese contains smaller areas called parishes. Each parish has its own religious leader, called a priest.

Most parishes include one church and a congregation, or group of regular worshippers. A parish priest has a very close relationship with his congregation. In many ways, they are similar to a shepherd and his flock, or a father and his children. In fact, priests are called "Father."

The main responsibilities of a priest include guiding his congregation in religious matters and conducting regular worship services. However, priests also perform many other duties. For instance, they supervise help for the needy, look after members of their congregation who are ill or troubled, organize fund-raising efforts, and oversee religious instruction such as Sunday school classes.

Priests share close relationships with the members of their congregations.

Only men can become priests. They go through many years of training. This schooling begins in high school or university. It usually continues for at least two years after university, in schools called seminaries. Typically, after years of service in a parish, a priest rises in the church structure. He can become a bishop or even rise to a higher office.

When a man becomes a priest, he takes several sacred vows. One is a vow of celibacy. *Celibacy* means not marrying or having sexual relations. Some priests also take a vow of poverty. This means rejecting money and material possessions.

Monks, Nuns, and Teaching Orders

Other important members of the Catholic Church's structure take similar vows of poverty and chastity. These are women called nuns and men called monks. They are unique to the Catholic religion.

Monks and nuns have existed since the earliest days of Catholicism. Like priests and bishops, they are part of a tradition that stretches back to the beginnings of the church. They devote themselves full-time to work, religious study, prayer, and service to others.

There are many different orders of monks and nuns. One of the most familiar is the Franciscan order. Franciscans are inspired by Saint Francis, who was a great advocate of peace. They are known for their involvement in issues of peace and justice.

In addition to monks and nuns, Catholicism has another unique form of religious leader. This is a set of religious groups called teaching orders. Teaching orders devote themselves to education and schools. One example of a teaching order is the Jesuits. The Jesuits operate many schools and universities around the world.

Acting on Their Beliefs

Some orders of nuns live in convents. Some orders of monks live in monasteries. These are spiritual retreats, far away from the everyday world. There they can devote themselves completely to solitary prayer, study, and occupations such as farming.

Nuns are unique to the Catholic religion. They can be found around the world helping others.

However, others are very involved in the affairs of the world. For instance, some operate schools, universities, missions, and hospitals. Some concentrate on helping the poor or disadvantaged by running food banks, homeless shelters, and other social services. Still others are active in political work. For instance, many members of Catholic religious orders are involved in the peace and justice movement. This is a loose group of organizations around the world that works to help oppressed people.

However, no matter what their duties might include, all of the members of the Catholic Church's structure have one primary duty. This is to foster and maintain faith in the practices of the church, guiding its many members along a spiritual path.

CHAPTER THREE

What Do I Believe?

All Catholics share certain beliefs. Some are also shared with other Christians, but many are unique to Catholicism.

Catholic beliefs are outlined in several sacred texts. These writings include the Old and New Testaments, which Catholics share with other Christians (and, in the case of the Old Testament, with Jews as well).

However, Catholicism also relies on many writings that are unique to it. In particular, there is the Catechism. This is a collection compiled by church leaders over many years to explain Catholic beliefs.

The Trinity

One of these basic beliefs, shared with most other Christians, concerns the Holy Trinity. This is the idea that God is one being but His divine presence is revealed in three ways.

The first part of the Trinity is God the Father, who is the creator of all things. The second is Jesus, the Son of God. The third is the Holy Spirit (sometimes called the Holy Ghost).

The Holy Spirit is God's constant and eternal presence in the world. The Spirit comforts and sustains people when they have hard times and helps them to always keep Jesus in their hearts.

A young girl studies the Catechism, a collection of writings that explain Catholic beliefs.

Catholics believe that God's presence is revealed through God the Father (top), Jesus (center), and the Holy Spirit, represented here as a dove (center).

Sin

Another basic belief concerns sin. A sin is a bad deed committed against a person or God. Catholicism places more importance on sin than most other forms of Christianity.

Catholic teaching recognizes two types of sin. One is mortal sin. Mortal sins are serious sins such as murder or not believing in God. The other type of sin, called venial sin, is less serious. For example, lying to another person or cheating is a venial sin. All sins require punishment. Committing a mortal sin can keep a person from going to Heaven after death. Venial sins require less serious punishment.

Some sins, such as murder and stealing, are also considered sins by Protestants and Jews. However, others are unique to the Catholic Church. Among these are abortion, artificial birth control, and divorce. Some Catholics are beginning to question whether some of these issues should really be considered sins. However, devout Catholics still obey the church's rulings on such matters.

Heaven and Hell

To be forgiven of sin is very important. Catholics believe that they can be cleansed of sin by believing in Jesus and asking for forgiveness from God. If they are forgiven, their immortal souls will go to Heaven. There they will be forever at peace and eternally close to God.

However, Catholics must do more than be forgiven to reach Heaven. They must also live good lives while they are on Earth. Living a good life includes keeping faith in God, showing love and compassion for others, performing good works, and personally correcting any sins they have committed.

Not everyone can do all this. It is therefore possible for a person's soul to be denied Heaven. According to

Catholicism, many people enter Purgatory after they die. This is a state where souls go to be cleansed of all sins before they can enter Heaven.

However, some souls will not even end up in Purgatory. Instead, they will go to an everlasting torment called Hell. Hell is ruled by devils, including Lucifer, an angel who fell from God's grace. According to Catholicism, God and the evil Lucifer are in constant battle to control humankind.

Miracles and Saints

Another basic Catholic belief concerns miracles. Miracles are wonderful events that have no natural explanations. Jesus performed many miracles, such as raising the dead, healing the sick, and feeding the poor. To Catholics, Jesus' triumph over death was the ultimate miracle.

Closely tied to belief in miracles is a belief in saints. Saints are people who have earned places of honor within Catholic belief. They are special because they led extraordinary lives, both as humans and as religious figures.

Saints have changed the world for the good in some way, such as devoting themselves to the poor. Some believed so completely in Catholicism that they willingly died for it at the hands of anti-Catholic torturers. All saints have also performed miracles verified by the church. For example, Saint Joan of Arc, who lived in the 1400s, is said to have cured three women of serious illnesses.

Young Catholics join hands in prayer. Catholics believe that prayer and good deeds will help their souls reach Heaven.

The Catholic Church frequently uses the term *patron saint.* A patron is someone who has special protective power. Patron saints may protect a country, a city, a group of people, or even animals. One example is Francis of Assisi. Saint Francis had a special relationship with all creatures, so he has become the patron saint of animals.

When Catholics pray, they pray only to the Holy Trinity. However, they can also ask for guidance from saints

Saint Francis of Assisi is the patron saint of animals. He had a special relationship with all creatures.

in certain situations. This request is called veneration. For example, Saint Jude is the patron saint of lost causes. Catholics who desperately need help with a hopeless situation often ask Saint Jude for guidance and aid.

Mary

The queen of all saints is Mary, Jesus' mother. Mary holds a special place in the Catholic Church because she was chosen by God to bear His Son. She has many loving names and titles, such as the Blessed Virgin. Over the centuries, Mary has achieved a place in Catholicism second only to Jesus.

When asking Mary for help, people use special sets of prayers dedicated to her. These prayers are repeated many times. People use strings of special beads, called rosary beads, to help them count how many prayers they have said.

As Jesus' mother, Mary holds a special place in the Catholic Church. She is also known as the Blessed Virgin.

Relics

Relics of saints are important to veneration. Sometimes these relics are parts of a saint's body, such as bones. Sometimes they are objects that have come into contact with a saint, such as clothing. Many Catholic churches, especially in Europe, display their precious relics with honor.

The Catholic Church has many thousands of saints, stretching from the beginnings of the church to modern times. The list grows all the time. However, the process of achieving sainthood is lengthy and complicated. For instance, the church must prove that the person has performed genuine miracles. Proving such things takes years of research.

Someone currently being considered for sainthood is Mother Teresa. Mother Teresa spent her life helping the poor in India and became one of the most beloved people in the world. The process to formally make her a saint began after her death in 1997. In 2003 Mother Teresa was beatified. This is one of the last major steps toward becoming a saint.

Venerating saints is just one part of Catholic worship. Many other ceremonies and rituals make up important parts of a Catholic's life.

CHAPTER FOUR

How Do I Practice My Faith?

C eremony is central to Catholicism. Its familiar patterns help Catholics feel connected to God and secure in their beliefs. Ritual also provides a strong sense of shared community with families and other church members.

Mass

The most important ceremony is Mass, the regular worship service. Some Catholics attend Mass only on Sundays and certain other holy days. Others go every day.

Attending Mass is another way in which Catholics differ from most other Christians. Only one other branch of Christianity, the Episcopalians, observes Mass.

The rituals of Mass are very old. Many can be traced back to the early days of Catholicism. Nonetheless, Mass has changed slightly over the centuries.

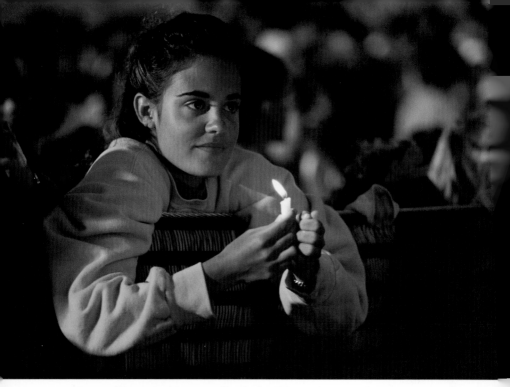

A worshipper holds a candle during Mass, the most important ceremony in Catholicism.

The biggest change concerns language. Until recently, Mass was held only in Latin, an ancient language. However, in the 1960s, many churches began using whatever languages were spoken in their particular countries.

Some Catholics object to this change and still attend churches that hold Latin Mass. They find the ancient language to be a beautiful link to the past.

Communion

Mass follows a very strict order. The first part includes songs or hymns and a prayer for forgiveness. It also includes readings from the Old Testament and the Gospels, a sermon by the priest, and a statement of faith called the Nicene Creed.

The second part of Mass centers on communion. Communion, also called the Eucharist or the Lord's Supper, is the most important part of the service.

During communion, people swallow special wafers and sip special wine. This echoes Jesus' last meal, when he blessed bread and wine and said, "This is my body. This is my blood. Do this in memory of me."

Catholics believe the wine and wafers miraculously become the body and blood of Jesus. By ingesting them, people maintain a direct connection with Jesus. They remember his teachings, his death, and his resurrection.

By taking communion, Catholics believe they maintain a direct connection with Jesus.

Baptism

There are many other Catholic ceremonies. The most important are called sacraments. Other Christian churches allow a few sacraments, usually baptism and communion. However, most are unique to Catholicism.

The sacraments are baptism, communion, confirmation, marriage, holy orders (special vows taken by priests), reconciliation, and anointing of the sick. Each marks an important moment in a Catholic's life.

The first is baptism, which initiates a person into Catholicism. This ritual began when John the Baptist used river water to baptize Jesus. It ritually washes away sins and symbolizes a new life in the kingdom of God.

Baptism initiates a person into Catholicism. Most people are baptized as babies.

Although baptism can be for adults becoming Catholics, typically it is performed at the age of about six weeks.

Baptism is joyous for a family. They welcome the new baby into their family and church, and formally give it a name. They also promise to raise the child as a Catholic. Traditionally, families ask friends to serve as godfathers or godmothers. These people will serve as role models and protectors in the future.

Communion and Confirmation

Communion takes place when children are about seven. In this ceremony, they take part fully for the first time in communion. A special Mass is held in their honor. From then on, they are expected to attend church and take communion at least weekly.

The next milestone is confirmation, which happens around age twelve. During this ceremony, young people renew their baptismal vows.

Confirmation represents a symbolic passing into adulthood. By taking part in confirmation, young people *choose* Catholicism.

Reconciliation

Baptism, communion, and confirmation are public rituals. People take part in them as part of the church community. However, other sacraments are private. For instance, there is reconciliation, or confession.

In reconciliation, a person confesses to sins and asks for forgiveness. A priest forgives the confessor in the

Reconciliation, or confession, is a private ritual when a person confesses to sins and asks for forgiveness from a priest.

name of God. He also assigns prayers, including special prayers called acts of contrition, for the person to say. Furthermore, the priest guides the confessor in promising God that the sin will not happen again, and in considering ways to become a better person.

Sometimes churches have booths with two compartments. The confessor is in one compartment, hidden from the priest. Sometimes the two meet face-to-face. In either case, the priest will never reveal a person's sins to anyone else.

Marriage and Death

The last sacraments concern marriage and death. For Catholics, like other Christians, marriage and family are seen as serious commitments. There are some differences, however. The church forbids divorce. This means that a Catholic marriage is a lifetime promise. Devout Catholics take this very seriously. Those who break their vows and seek divorce can be asked to leave the church.

The final ritual in a person's life is called anointing of

For Catholics, marriage is a lifetime promise. The Catholic Church forbids divorce.

the sick. In this, a priest blesses an ill or wounded person and forms a cross with oil. This symbolically heals the person, forgives sins, and prepares the way for entry into Heaven.

Originally, this ceremony was called last rites and was only for people close to dying. Today, it is viewed as a healing ritual. Seriously ill or frail people can receive it, even if they are not close to death.

CHAPTER FIVE

What Holidays Do I Celebrate?

L ike all religions, Catholicism has many holidays throughout the year. It shares some of these, such as Christmas and Easter, with other branches of Christianity. However, many holidays are unique to Catholicism, such as the feast days of saints.

Lent

The most important holiday time in the Catholic religious calendar is the Lent/Easter season in the spring. Easter celebrates Jesus' resurrection. This is his miraculous triumph over death and ascent into Heaven. Easter's exact date is determined by the moon, not the sun, so it can come as early as March 22 or as late as April 25.

The forty days leading up to Easter are called Lent. Although other Christians celebrate Easter, Lent is largely a Catholic tradition. It begins with Ash Wednesday. On

On Ash Wednesday, priests mark Catholics' foreheads with a cross of ashes to represent the cycle of life and death.

this day priests mark the foreheads of people with a cross of ashes. This recalls the Bible's mention of the cycle of life and death.

Another important day for Catholics during the season of Lent is Palm Sunday. On this day, people go to church for a special service that includes the distribution of palm leaves to the congregation. The palm leaves recall the time when Jesus rode a donkey into Jerusalem, and people along the way waved palm leaves (a symbol of victory) to welcome him.

Easter

Throughout Lent, Catholics make a special effort to think about their sins and ask God to forgive them. They also give up something that they like. This sacrifice is usually done in order to perform some good deed. For example, a person might give up eating in restaurants and instead donate the money to charity. Making a sacrifice can thus make a Catholic into a better, more sympathetic person.

Lent ends on Holy Thursday with a special Mass. It is followed by Good Friday. Good Friday recalls the day when Jesus died on the cross. On this solemn day, churches are stripped of excess decorations, and people attend only a simple service. Many people fast as well, in order to honor Jesus' hardships.

On the following day, Holy Saturday, Catholics attend a special evening or nighttime service called a vigil. The ceremonies during the vigil recall the resurrection of Jesus. They include lighting a special candle to symbolize Jesus' passing from death to everlasting life.

On Holy Saturday, Catholics attend a special service to celebrate the resurrection of Jesus.

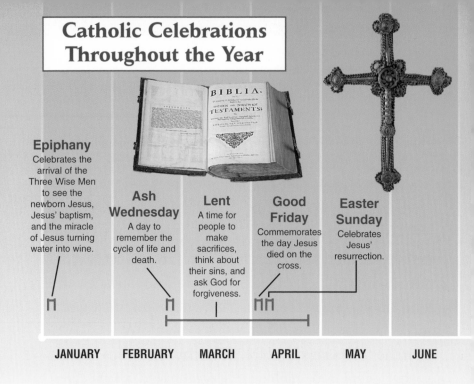

Catholic Celebrations Throughout the Year

Epiphany
Celebrates the arrival of the Three Wise Men to see the newborn Jesus, Jesus' baptism, and the miracle of Jesus turning water into wine.

Ash Wednesday
A day to remember the cycle of life and death.

Lent
A time for people to make sacrifices, think about their sins, and ask God for forgiveness.

Good Friday
Commemorates the day Jesus died on the cross.

Easter Sunday
Celebrates Jesus' resurrection.

JANUARY   FEBRUARY   MARCH   APRIL   MAY   JUNE

Then comes Easter Sunday. This day honors the resurrection of Jesus and his ascent into Heaven. A special Mass is held on this holiest of days. It includes the joyful words "Christ is risen."

Advent

Next in importance for Catholics is the Advent/Christmas season in the winter. Christmas honors the birth of Jesus. Catholics share many of its observances and traditions with other Christians.

Christmas falls on December 25, which is traditionally the day of Jesus' birth. This exact date has never been pinpointed. However, Christmas has been celebrated by the Catholic Church on December 25 since A.D. 350.

The four weeks before Christmas are called Advent. Like Lent, it is largely a Catholic tradition. In part, this

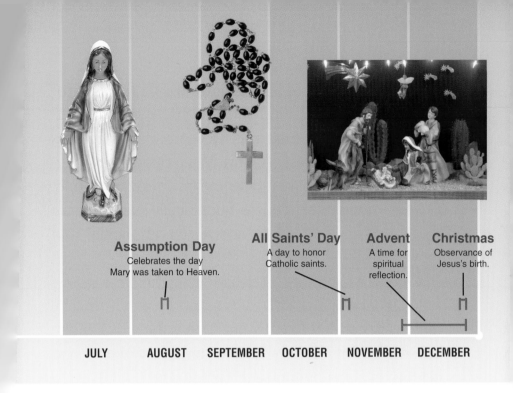

Assumption Day
Celebrates the day
Mary was taken to Heaven.

All Saints' Day
A day to honor
Catholic saints.

Advent
A time for
spiritual
reflection.

Christmas
Observance of
Jesus's birth.

JULY   AUGUST   SEPTEMBER   OCTOBER   NOVEMBER   DECEMBER

is a time for spiritual reflection. Catholics try especially hard to follow Jesus' example of compassion and generosity. For example, they may help those who are less fortunate by contributing to charities, volunteering in homeless shelters, or performing other acts of penance.

However, Advent is also a joyful time, when people hold parties, attend musical or theatrical performances about Christmas, or decorate their houses. One familiar custom is to decorate evergreen trees, under which family members and friends put presents for each other.

Christmas

Santa Claus has long been part of the Christmas tradition as well. The legend of Santa and his custom of giving gifts to children began with a fourth-century saint, Nicholas of Myra. Nicholas set an example of quiet, generous giving to the poor.

However, the real meaning of Christmas for Catholics is the holy and solemn observance of Jesus' birth. Late on Christmas Eve, December 24, Catholics attend a special Mass. At this Mass, people hear sermons about what Jesus' birth means in today's world. On Christmas Day, people traditionally eat a special meal, exchange presents, and visit with family and friends.

Catholics continue to celebrate the Christmas season until January 6. This holiday is called Epiphany. It celebrates three events in Jesus' life. One is the arrival of the Three Wise Men to see the newborn Jesus. The second is Jesus' baptism by John the Baptist. The third event is

Catholics attend a special Mass on Christmas Eve to learn what Jesus' birth means in today's world.

the miracle that took place when Jesus turned water into wine at a marriage feast.

Holy Days for Mary and Saints

Many other holidays occur throughout the year. In fact, almost every day of the calendar is special in one way or another to Catholics.

For example, there are certain days besides each Sunday on which Catholics must attend Mass. These are called holy days of obligation. They vary from country to country. One is All Saints' Day on November 1. On this day Catholics honor all the saints, especially those without special feast days.

There are several days throughout the year that are devoted to Mary. One of these is August 15, Assumption Day. It celebrates the day when, according to Catholic belief, Mary was taken to Heaven.

In addition, all around the world various countries, cities, and ethnic groups hold festivals on days devoted to individual saints. For example, every September millions of people attend a colorful street fair held by New York City's Italian American community. It honors San Gennaro (Saint Januarius), the patron saint of Naples, who has been adopted by many Italian Americans as their patron. Such festivals and holidays represent the many ways in which Catholics continue to express a deep and lasting faith in their ancient religion.

FOR FURTHER EXPLORATION

Books

Carole Armstrong, *Lives and Legends of the Saints.* New York: Simon & Schuster, 1995. This book is beautifully illustrated with classic paintings of some of the major saints.

Michael Keane, *What You Will See Inside a Catholic Church.* Woodstock, VT: Skylight Paths, 2002. Using photographs, this book clearly explains some of the major ideas of Catholicism and the meanings of the many parts of a church.

Brenda Pettenuzzo, *I Am a Roman Catholic.* New York and London: Franklin Watts, 1985. A young British Catholic girl is profiled in this book.

Philemon D. Sevastiades, *I Am Roman Catholic.* New York: Rosen, 1996. A very simple introduction.

Web sites

Catholic Courier.com (www.catholiccourier.com). An online magazine that has a section, "Kids' Chronicle," with puzzles, Bible stories, and more.

Catholic Kids' Net (www.catholickidsnet.org/kidsonly. html). This site has lots of ways for kids to learn about Catholicism, including lives of the saints and a featured kid artist of the month.

St. Jude Coloring Book (http://cweb.snip.net/stjude/ colorbk.htm). This site has scenes, ready for printing and coloring, leading kids through the steps of a Catholic Mass.

The Young Saints Club (www.geocities.com/Athens/ 1619). A monthly online newsletter for Catholic kids, with stories, prayers, games, and more.

INDEX

INDEX

PICTURE CREDITS

ABOUT THE AUTHOR

Adam Woog is the author of many books for adults, young adults, and children. He grew up in Seattle, Washington, and lives there with his wife and daughter.